PLIMOTH PLANTATION

A Pictorial Guide

Photography by Plimoth Plantation
Introduction and Text by James W. Baker

Plimoth Plantation, Plymouth, Massachusetts

Mayflower master Christopher Jones and his officers used charts such as John Smith's to navigate in New England waters.

After a month at Cape Cod, *Mayflower* (towing the shallop) sailed into Plymouth Harbor on December 16, 1620.

The Story of the Pilgrims

The story of the Pilgrims and their Indian neighbors is familiar to most Americans, and many international visitors as well. It evokes powerful images of strength in the face of adversity, of ships on storm-tossed oceans and winters on bleak New England shores; yet, also of harvest plenty, of Thanksgiving gatherings and golden autumnal afternoons. However, the historic reality which underlies this greeting card imagery is far more complex. The colonists who arrived in 1620 brought not only European tools and technology, but also hopes, dreams and a Christian faith reflecting a decidedly seventeenth-century English view of the world. The Native People, the Wampanoag, had their own complex society which did not comfortably coexist with that of their new English neighbors. Plimoth Plantation,

Crewmen aboard seventeenth-century ships ate a dull diet of dried and salted food prepared by boiling it in the ship's cookroom.

While at sea, passengers often had to attend to their own food, which they cooked over small portable charcoal braziers.

through its innovative living history programs, brings the fascinating story of these two very different societies to life.

In the winter of 1620, a group of English colonists arrived at Cape Cod intending to create a permanent settlement. The core members of this immigrant group were Separatists, members of a reformed sect from the Scrooby area of Nottinghamshire which had split away from the established Church of England. This move was considered treasonous by the Crown, and they were persecuted by King James I's royal officials. As a consequence the Separatists fled to the more tolerant Netherlands.

For twelve years the Separatists lived in the city of Leiden, where they were able to gather openly as a church under minister John Robinson. However, life in a foreign country was not without problems. The only occupations open to most immigrants were poorly paid, and they found themselves growing old in poverty. The twelve-year truce between Holland and Spain was to end in 1621, threatening a resumption of hostilities. Also troublesome to the Separatists were the hardships endured by their young people, who were forced by circumstance to work at exceptionally hard jobs. Others were assimilated into the Dutch culture, leaving their parents and their community profoundly disturbed.

A group of English investors known as the "merchant adventurers" financed the voyage and settlement. They formed a joint-stock company with the colonists in which the merchants agreed to "adventure" (risk) their money, and the settlers to invest their personal labor, for a period of seven years. During that time, all land and livestock were to be owned in partnership; afterwards the company would be dissolved and the assets divided.

A square-rigged vessel such as *Mayflower* required sailors to go aloft to tend the great linen canvas sails.

The famous "Mayflower Compact" was signed by 41 men in Cape Cod (Provincetown) Harbor, November 11, 1620.

To help ensure the colony's success the merchants recruited additional emigrants to join with the Leiden contingent. Although strangers to the Leiden congregation, the newcomers were equal partners in the new colonizing venture. The Leiden group bought a small ship, *Speedwell*, for the voyage and later use in America. They sailed to England in July 1620, where they met the other colonists and a larger hired vessel, *Mayflower*, at Southampton. Preparations and negotiations with the London merchants were completed by August 5th when the two ships set sail for the New World. Unfortunately, the *Speedwell* leaked badly, forcing the ships to turn back twice. Leaving the *Speedwell* behind at Plymouth, England, *Mayflower* went on alone on September 6th. The colonists were headed for the mouth of the Hudson River, near the northern boundary of the Virginia colony.

After a voyage of 66 days, *Mayflower* arrived safely off Cape Cod on November 9th. Because winter was setting in and travel through the Cape's outer shoals was dangerous, the colonists decided to settle in New England. As this was outside of the territory in which their patent or license to settle was valid, they signed an agreement (the "Mayflower Compact") on November 11th to work together to build their own colony. Leaving *Mayflower* anchored off what is now Provincetown, exploring parties set out aboard their shallop (a small work boat) in search of a suitable place for settlement. They chose a site twenty-six miles to the west across Cape Cod Bay, which English explorer Captain John Smith had named "Plimouth" on his 1614 map of New England. Arriving at this harbor in a storm, the shallop crew spent two days on Clark's Island before landing at their future home on December 11, 1620. This area had been abandoned by the Patuxet Indians, who had nearly all died several years earlier of European diseases.

The "First Encounter" between the *Mayflower* colonists and Native Americans at Eastham on Cape Cod in December, 1620, was violent, but no one was harmed.

The Wampanoag had lived in southern New England for thousands of years, and were highly skilled in such crafts as the construction of *mishoon* or dug-out canoes.

Half the colonists and crew died of sickness brought on by malnutrition and exposure during the winter of 1620/21. Living aboard *Mayflower*, they began construction of their homes and storehouses on December 23, 1620. During their work, they were surprised to be greeted in English by Samoset, a Native American from Maine. He introduced the colonists to a survivor of the Patuxet named Squanto, who became their resident guide and interpreter in dealing with the other Native Peoples of New England. When *Mayflower* returned to England on April 5, 1621, none of the colonists went back. They planted their crops, made a treaty of friendship with sachem Massasoit and other leaders of the Wampanoag Indians, and enjoyed a successful harvest in the fall of 1621. Other ships arrived in the following years bringing goods, livestock and additional colonists. Plimoth Plantation grew and prospered.

Colonists who arrived on the three subsequent ships, together with Plymouth births, swelled the colony's population to over 150 people by 1627, three times that of 1621. Many other changes occurred in the first seven years as well. The merchant adventurers broke up in 1624, leaving the colonists in debt and in need of alternative financial support. Unable to make their living through cod fishing as they had originally planned, the colonists turned to agriculture and trade instead. The Plantation's chief crop, Indian corn, was traded with the Native Americans to the north for highly valued beaver skins, These were profitably sold in England to pay the colony's debts and buy necessary supplies.

1: *Mayflower* II in Provincetown Harbor at the tip of
Cape Cod, where the first *Mayflower* anchored in 1620.
2: The master of the *Mayflower* trains the Ship's Boy
in use of a quadrant and cross staff for determining
the vessel's latitude.

1: A woman sits sewing on the hatch gratings. Passengers were expected to go above decks from their "cabbins" for air and exercise.

2: Two seamen work to raise the anchor. The anchor cable was wound on the horizontal wooden winch or "windlass" and dropped into the forward hold.

3: Mayflower II unfurls her linen sails to dry and air them at the State Pier in Plymouth, Massachusetts.

1: The master of the *Mayflower* takes his ease in the Great Cabin, sharing a drink with one of his men.

2: Passengers aboard *Mayflower* were crowded below decks where they had small "cabbins"—cubicles or bunks—where they spent much of their time aboard ship.

3: The aftercastle in the stern of the *Mayflower* displays the tarred standing rigging which supports the main and mizzen masts.

2

3

1: The colonists' shallop or work boat had a shallow draft for coastal waters, and could be propelled by sail or oars.

2: Mayflower's crewmen prepare to furl and fasten the main and fore "courses" or sails on their yards.

A New Plymouth housewife uses a ceramic watering device to gently sprinkle the flourishing herbs and flowers in the kitchen garden beside her home.

Use of the substantial "great" chair was reserved for the father of the family and head of the household.

The 1627 Pilgrim Village

Plimoth Plantation's Pilgrim Village brings to life the Plymouth of 1627. This year was selected because it is well-documented and represents the village just before the colonists began to disperse beyond the first settlement. Seven years after the arrival of *Mayflower*, "The Street" rises westward from Plymouth Harbor to the Fort/Meetinghouse on the hill. It replicates the original site of the Plymouth settlement, which is today Leyden Street in downtown Plymouth. Most of the houses are located on either side of this street. Crossing near the center of the Street is "the highway" which runs north and south to the cornfields. In today's 1627 Pilgrim Village, the houses on the north side of the Street (from the east end) represent the homes of the Soule, Annable, Fuller, Howland, Hopkins, Bradford, Alden and Standish families. On the south side are storehouses, the common house, and the Browne, Brewster, Billington, Allerton, Cooke and Winslow houses. Community structures such as the cow house, hay house and outdoor oven are found throughout the village.

The Fort/Meetinghouse dominates the hillside on which the village is located. It is a timber-framed blockhouse, with a ground floor meeting area and an upper gundeck overlooking the surrounding landscape. Enclosing both the Fort/Meetinghouse and the village is a palisade, a defensive barrier made of split or riven logs with bulwarks and gates at the corners. The colony built these defenses in 1622 upon news of the massacre of colonists in Virginia. The fortification was intended to protect the town from assault by the Indian nations or England's French and Spanish enemies. Fortunately, attack never came, and the Fort/Meetinghouse was used as a meeting place for religious services and as a court-

Children in New Plymouth received their education within the family setting, whether the lesson was reading and writing or how to prepare a meal.

Cattle played an important role in the life of New Plymouth, not only for "white meats" (dairy products) but also to fertilize the surrounding fields.

house for the colony's legislative and judicial affairs.

Gazing eastward from the Fort/Meetinghouse visitors are struck by the dramatic vista, in which the earthy tones of the village are set off against the deep blue of Cape Cod Bay. The double row of thatched and clapboarded houses reflect the vernacular building tradition of rural England and the colonists' varied backgrounds. They range in type from hovels—simple A-frame temporary dwellings—to more substantial structures an early visitor to Plymouth Colony described as "very fair and pleasant."

Each house contains painstakingly accurate reproductions of the furniture, tools, and cooking equipment representing the material possessions listed in Plymouth probate inventories. They are not just for display, but are used by the museum staff to re-create the daily life of the colony. The activities of the settlement, all appropriate to the changing seasons, are carried out in the correct seventeenth-century manner. The 1627 Plantation was above all a farming community, and the working day for today's "villagers" is largely taken up by agricultural or foodways tasks. However,

life in Plymouth Colony was not all work and no play. Special times such as births, weddings, militia musters and successful harvests gathered the community for socializing, feasting and even games.

Clothed in period fashions and speaking in the accents of their character's place of origin, museum staff—"interpreters"—take on the identities of the original inhabitants of the colony. Together, these "first person" roles replicate the social and cultural life of a real human community. The housewife's primary daily responsibility was feeding and caring for her household. The primary occupation of Plymouth men was farming, although many had training in trades such as coopering or blacksmithing which became part-time occupations. The village shelters seventeenth-century breeds of cattle, goats, sheep, swine and poultry, many of which are quite rare today. Outside the palisade are fields which produce the crops that were the Pilgrims' major source of food. Adjacent to each house are kitchen gardens for both food and medicine.

1: Two men thatch a new roof while another man works on daubing the inside of a timber-framed chimney.

2: An oaken log is "riven" (split) using a wooden maul and wedges to make furniture, clapboards or barrel staves.

3: A New Plymouth housewife takes advantage of the daylight outside of her house to make repairs to a garment.

2

3

1: Some corn was saved on the ear to use as seed for the following season. One kernel of corn could return two or three ears.

2: New Plymouth girls work to husk and braid ears of corn for winter storage. Drying and husking corn occupied many hours in the fall and winter.

3: In one of the most famous episodes of Plymouth history, Tisquantum (Squanto) shows the Pilgrims how to fertilize corn mounds with "herring" (alewives).

1: Like their Wampanoag counterparts, New Plymouth
women contributed to the supplies of food by gathering
shellfish at low tide.

2: Four men using English muskets were able in one day
to provide enough wild fowl to supply the participants
at the "First Thanksgiving" for several days.

3: A New Plymouth housewife plucks a wild turkey in
preparation for a bountiful fall dinner.

By 1627, New Plymouth was flourishing, blessed with good gardens, solid thatched and clapboarded houses, a growing store of livestock and a population of about 150 persons.

1: All water used in New Plymouth had to be carried from springs that flowed into the Town Brook.

2: A New Plymouth housewife grinds herbs and seasonings in a brass mortar for later mixing into pork meat for sausages.

3: The New Plymouth blacksmith works at the community forge to fashion small ironware such as hinges and fasteners for village usage.

2

3

1: While a man cuts the ripe grain, two New Plymouth women gather and bind the harvest sheaves.

2: A New Plymouth roof is thatched with bundles of dried cattail reeds.

1: Seven years after the arrival of the *Mayflower*,
"The Street" rises westward from Plymouth Harbor
to the Fort/Meetinghouse on the hill.

2: In the spring of the year, the raised garden beds
are planted and "herring" (alewives) can be dip-netted
in the brook below the village.

3: The Elder of the New Plymouth church,
William Brewster, brought a library of several hundred
titles in several languages to America.

1

2

1: A New Plymouth child is shown how to feed the young goats. Both boys and girls wore skirts until about six years of age.

2: A New Plymouth man fixes the burning matchcord into the serpentine of his matchlock musket in preparation to fire.

3: A squad of the New Plymouth militia practice their military skills. They are using matchlock muskets and wear bandoliers of wooden powder charges.

1: Now famous as the "First Thanksgiving," the harvest celebration of 1621 brought the English and the Wampanoag together for three days of celebration.

2: A New Plymouth housewife prepares a simple dish for the dinner meal.

Overleaf: Outdoor work, whether gathering fuel or bringing water to the livestock, goes on in New Plymouth despite winter weather.

A Wampanoag woman fashions a coiled-clay pot in the manner of her ancestors. It will later be "brush-fired" to make it ready for cooking.

The exchange of fur pelts for cloth, iron tools and other European goods played a major role in the early interaction between the two New England cultures.

Hobbamock's Wampanoag Indian Homesite

In Hobbamock's Homesite a very different culture from that of the Pilgrim Village is depicted. On this carefully re-created Native farm, interpreters discuss the Native Peoples who lived in southeastern New England in the seventeenth century. The encampment represents the home of a particular Wampanoag family, that of the Pokanoket *pniese* (warrior-counselor) Hobbamock, who lived just south of the Plymouth settlement in the early seventeenth century.

The interpreters in Hobbamock's Homesite do not take on character roles as in the 1627 Pilgrim Village but explain Wampanoag culture from a modern perspective through conversation, craft activities and storytelling. Staff who are Native Americans dress in the deerskins and trade cloth garments of their ancestors.

The name "Wampanoag" means "eastern people," or "people of the dawn." Some of these Native Peoples still live on or near the fields, forests and waters where their ancestors settled thousands of years ago. In the seventeenth century they were known by the names of their separate territories, such as Pokanoket, Patuxet and Nauset. Each community had authority over a well-defined territory from which the People derived their livelihood through a seasonal round of fishing, planting, harvesting and hunting. The Wampanoag way

Native American men had far greater success in hunting deer using traditional methods than the English had with their muskets in the first days of the colony.

The Wampanoag made use of the many natural resources of their homeland, such as sumac flowers from which both a drink flavoring and a dye could be extracted.

of life fostered an harmonious relationship between the People and their natural environment, both physical and spiritual. They were united by a common language and a shared respect for the traditions and the elders of their nation.

The work of making a living was organized on a family level. At times families gathered together, as in the spring to fish or in early winter to hunt, and in the summer they separated to cultivate individual planting fields. Boys were schooled in the ways of the woods, where a man's skill at hunting and ability to survive under all conditions were vital to his family's well-being. Native women were trained from girlhood to work diligently in the fields and around the family *wetu*.

In Hobbamock's Homesite, there are two *wetus*—houses built of curved saplings covered with bark or woven cattail mats. The larger dwelling or *nees quttow*, is appropriate for an important man such as Hobbamock. The interior walls are covered with fine bulrush mats, which are decorative and provide insulation. The more elaborate mats include dyed rushes. Within the *wetus* are the typical possessions of

a Native family, many of which are for obtaining and storing food. There are also a few European trade goods such as iron pots and tools. The only furnishings are the built-in sleeping platforms covered with skins.

The adjacent gardens were originally cleared by cutting and burning the trees and shrubs. Overlooked by a "corn-watch," a raised platform from which plants could be guarded from birds, the plots are planted with the traditional crops of corn, beans and squash. These crops were cultivated by women and children, while men grew tobacco separately. Women's activities included gathering wild foodstuffs, cooking, tanning hides and making the clothing, mats, baskets, bags and pottery used in the household. The men hunted, fished, and made intricate objects and tools out of stone and wood, such as arrows, axes, canoes, bowls and spoons.

1: The *nees quttow* (house with two fires) in Hobbamock's Homesite is rebuilt with new cedar poles before the bark cladding is put on to the frame.
2: A raccoon cloak brings welcome warmth to a Wampanoag woman on a cold, New England winter's day.

1: The mat-covered *puttuckakaun* or "round house" and the cooking arbor can be seen over the summer's crop of corn at Hobbamock's Homesite.

2: Two Native American men dress in the styles of the Wampanoag at the time of the arrival of the Pilgrims.

Mayflower II was built at the Upham shipyard in Brixham, Devonshire. Her timbers are hewn of English oak, and fastened with wooden "trunnels."

Mayflower II was launched on September 22, 1956, and sailed to Dartmouth and Plymouth, England, before beginning her trans-Atlantic crossing in April, 1957.

Mayflower II

Mayflower II is berthed near Plymouth Rock, three miles north of Plimoth Plantation's Eel River site. A full-scale reproduction of the type of early seventeenth-century merchant vessel that brought the Pilgrims to America, the three-masted *Mayflower II* is a small ship by today's standards: 106½ feet long, with a beam of 25½ feet and a draft of 13 feet. Naval architect William A. Baker began developing plans of the ship for Plimoth Plantation in 1951. In 1955, the Plantation was approached by Warwick Charlton of Project Mayflower, Ltd., an English group which wanted to build a reproduction of the *Mayflower* and sail it to America in recognition of the two nations' historic ties. Plimoth Plantation allowed Project Mayflower to use the Baker plans, and agreed to care for the vessel after she arrived in Plymouth, Massachusetts. Construction began at the Upham shipyard in Brixham, England on July 4, 1955. Great care was taken to use historically accurate materials such as English oak timbers, linen canvas sails, and true hemp rope. In 1957,

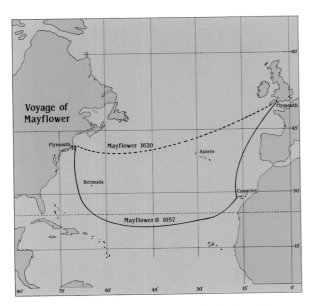

This map shows the route by which the first *May-flower* came to America in 1620, and the more southerly route followed by *Mayflower II* in 1957.

Mayflower II was greeted by thousands of well-wishers on June 13, 1957, including Vice-President Richard Nixon.

Mayflower II sailed across the Atlantic under the command of Captain Alan Villiers, arriving at Plymouth on June 13 after a 55-day voyage. *Mayflower II* was opened to the public at the State Pier in Plymouth the following year.

Since 1958, Plimoth Plantation has exhibited *Mayflower II* to tell the story of the famous 1620 voyage and the terrible "first winter" in which half of the first *Mayflower's* passengers and crew died from exposure and malnutrition. By the spring of 1620/21, the Pilgrims had built several houses in their new village, and had moved most of their possessions and people ashore. Hope for the success of the new colony ran strong. For the passengers, the two-month voyage was now a vivid memory of a tedious yet frightening experience. Their impressions might be contrasted with those of the seasoned crewmen who were preparing the vessel for the return voyage to England.

The crew was responsible for the performance of the ship, including navigation and sailing. To the rear of the half-deck is the poop cabin, which housed the charts and navigational instruments by which the ship's position and course were determined.

At sea, the man on watch gave orders through the conning hatch by the mizzen mast to the helmsman below in Steerage. He in turn steered the assigned course by the use of a whipstaff (a predecessor of the wheel) and the two compasses housed in the binnacle. On a normal voyage, the ship's officers bunked in the Steerage area, and the Great Cabin, behind the whipstaff, was quarters for the ship's master. Most of the crew slept "before the mast" in the fo'c'sle, which also served as the ship's cookroom.

Although not a naval vessel, *Mayflower* carried several cannon in the 'Tween Decks area for defense. It was there that most of the 102 passengers were housed on the 1620 voyage in small "cabbins" built along the sides of the ship. Their personal possessions, except for the minimum needed for daily existence, were stowed below in the hold with the ship's stores until they were brought ashore at Plymouth.

A member of the *Mayflower II* Maritime Artisans replaces the planking on the port side of the after-castle.

Plants used on the Plantation grounds, from Pilgrim Village gardens to decorations at the Visitor Center are the Horticultural Department's responsibility.

Behind-the-Scenes

The success of the public programs and exhibits at Plimoth Plantation depends in a large part on the knowledge and skills of behind-the-scenes staff who work to re-create the past. While not always apparent to the visitor, their efforts to painstakingly discover and restore each period detail make *Mayflower II*, the 1627 Pilgrim Village, and Hobbamock's Homesite the successful living history exhibits they are today. Re-creating Plymouth Colony's past requires investigation into all aspects of the two relevant cultures, English and Wampanoag. Drawing on evidence and information from our growing library of research materials and collections of period English, Dutch and Wampanoag artifacts, staff members work to devise detailed and accurate historical environments and provide costumed interpreters with information about the life and times of the people they are representing. Interpreter train-

All of the reproduction clothing worn by the Colonial Interpretation Department is made by the tailors and seamstresses in the Wardrobe Department.

The skill of the role players in Plimoth Plantation's unique "first person" living history program sets the museum apart from other outdoor exhibits.

ing is extensive and ongoing, and includes lectures, workshops and directed studies.

Most of the physical objects seen in our open air exhibits, from the Pilgrim Village houses to the deerskin Native clothes, are created by the Plantation staff. Whether working behind the scenes, in the Carriage House Crafts Center or in costume alongside the interpretive staff, curatorial artisans and craftspeople build and maintain the physical elements of the living history sites. "Living artifacts" such as historical crops, plants and rare breed livestock are maintained in the Maxwell Agricultural Center and in the Plimoth Plantation Horticulture Center. The gardens, livestock and corn fields are all products of the coordinated efforts of the Agricultural and Horticultural departments and the Colonial Interpretation or Wampanoag Indian Program staffs. Together, research, training and craftsmanship combine to give the visitor a unique opportunity—the chance to travel in time and visit the past.

Living History

Living history, a relative newcomer to the museum field, represents and interprets an historical situation contextually, combining people, livestock, plants and material culture within a reproduction of the physical environment which originally supported them. To accomplish this, an entire culture needs to be investigated and understood—what the inhabitants thought of their world, their hopes and fears, and how they interacted with their environment.

The interpretive staff in Hobbamock's Homesite employ a twentieth century, or "third-person" perspective, as they talk about what people used to do. "First-person interpretation" as presented in the 1627 Pilgrim Village goes one step further. The interpreters assume historical identities to become living artifacts within the re-created environment. Both methods help provide the visitor with a fuller understanding of the Plymouth colonists and their Wampanoag neighbors.

A Carriage House Crafts Center potter creates the reproductions that are used in the Pilgrim Village, which can also be purchased in the museum shop.

Plimoth Plantation's Rare and Minor Breeds program replicates Plymouth Colony's livestock, using Arapawa Island goats, similar to the now extinct Old English goats.

Carriage House Crafts Center

A major attraction at most open air-museums are the craftspeople at work in the historical areas. Unfortunately, Plimoth Plantation cannot exhibit crafts in the outdoor exhibits. There were few trades being practiced in 1627 Plymouth Colony, and the colonists relied on imports of manufactured articles for many of their needs. Today the Crafts Center serves as the source of "imports" into the Pilgrim Village and *Mayflower II* exhibits, and visitors may also buy the items they see being reproduced. A replica of the facade of the fifteenth-century guild hall in Thaxted, England, divides the introductory gallery exhibit explaining the importance of trade and commerce to Plymouth Colony from the workshops of our craft artisans who can be seen hard at work creating pottery, shoemaking, working at basketry or wood joinery.

The Nye Barn

The Nye Barn is a modern facility which allows visitors an in-depth look at our Rare and Minor Breeds Animal Program. Located between the Peabody Pavilion and the Bus/Handicapped Parking Lot, this oak timber frame structure has three stalls with access to a double fenced pasture and an exhibition area. There is also a graphic display of photographs and texts explaining the history of the various breeds of livestock exhibited at Plimoth Plantation.

Plimoth Plantation's livestock collections include Milking Devon and Kerry cattle, Arapawa and San Clemente Island goats, wild and Tamworth swine, Wiltshire Horned sheep, Dorking fowl and eastern wild turkeys, representing the types of animals which were found in Plymouth Colony in the seventeenth century. Many of these animals have been classified as having critically low breeding populations by the American Livestock Breed Conservancy. Plimoth Plantation has taken on an important responsibility for maintaining genetic diversity in modern livestock while also adhering to the high level of historical accuracy critical to the Plantation program.

In addition to video and interactive computer technology, *Irreconcilable Differences* uses a variety of objects and texts to tell the later Plymouth Colony story.

Brownescombe's idyllic "The First Thanksgiving" (ca. 1914) depicts the familiar modern image of the Pilgrims as symbols of the American Thanksgiving holiday.

Irreconcilable Differences

Irreconcilable Differences 1620 - 1692 is an interactive exhibit which explores the history of Plymouth Colony over the 72 years of its existence from both Wampanoag Indian and English viewpoints. Installed in the Shelby Cullom Davis Exhibition Galleries in the Hornblower Visitor Center, the exhibit uses video and interactive computer technology to allow visitors to experience the seventeenth century through the eyes of *Mayflower* passenger Mary Allerton Cushman (1616-1699) and Wampanoag Squaw Sachem Awashonks (ca. 1620-1684). Their stories accompany visitors through ten settings as history unfolds. Four of the rooms are re-created period interiors, including the 1620 storehouse, a 1680's gaol cell, two rooms from the 1680's Rickard "ordinary" or inn, and an entire Wampanoag *nees qutow* or "house with two fires."

    Irreconcilable Differences helps counter the criticism leveled at living history sites — that by focusing on a single moment in time, they ignore cultural change and continuity. In this exhibit Plimoth Plantation investigates such topics as the social construction of race, the intersection of Native and English economies over time, later century craft activities, changes in Native and colonial demographics, the period role of women, foodways, political life and religious belief.

Pilgrim Myths and Realities

Plimoth Plantation's founder, Harry Hornblower II, once observed that "the difficulty of the Pilgrim Story is that there are really two stories—a true historical one and a romantic one." Plimoth Plantation is dedicated to the genuine history of Plymouth Colony, but the cultural importance of the romance of "the Pilgrim Fathers" must be acknowledged as well. Without the Pilgrims, our Thanksgiving holiday would be unrecognizable, and there would be no Plimoth Plantation at all. Stories of the Landing on Plymouth Rock, the romantic triangle of John Alden, Priscilla Mullins and Myles Standish, or the First Thanksgiving have had too strong an influence on our national culture to be ignored.

    These famous fictions, while based on real traditions and actual events, do not reflect what actually happened in the past. They are instead expressions of the national values and shared experiences that have defined American society over the past two centuries. New national myths and traditions are evolving even now, but we need to appreciate the role of the heroic Pilgrim Story in order to better understand the society we live in today.

The Museum

Plimoth Plantation, Inc., is a private, non-profit living history museum. It is located 45 miles south of Boston in historic Plymouth, Massachusetts. Founded in 1947, the museum has grown from one small re-created house on the Plymouth waterfront to include three major open-air exhibits featuring live interpretation —the 1627 Pilgrim Village, Hobbamock's Wampanoag Indian Homesite, and *Mayflower II*—as well as other facilities, exhibits and programs. Near the Pilgrim Village stands the Carriage House Crafts Center, a modern facility housing an exhibition gallery, period crafts exhibition area and crafts shop. *Mayflower II* and the J. Barnes Bake Shop are located near Plymouth Rock on the Plymouth waterfront. The 1627 Pilgrim Village, Hobbamock's Homesite, Carriage House Crafts Center and Hornblower Visitor Center are three miles south on Route 3A at Plimoth Plantation's Eel River site. Support facilities at the Hornblower Visitor Center include theaters, exhibition galleries, food service and dining areas, and several museum shops.

Plimoth Plantation takes the spelling of its name from Gov. Bradford's most common usage, which serves to differentiate the museum from the original Plymouth Colony or Plantation and the present Town of Plymouth.

Credits:

Photography and Text © copyright 1997 by Plimoth Plantation

Book © copyright 1997 by Fort Church Publishers, Inc.

This book, or portions thereof, may not be reproduced in any manner without permission in writing of Fort Church Publishers, Inc.

Photographs and Text may not be reproduced in any manner without the written permission of Plimoth Plantation

Designed by Donald G. Paulhus

Published by Fort Church Publishers, Inc.
Little Compton, R.I. 02837

Printed in Japan

Distributed by Plimoth Plantation, 137 Warren Avenue, Plymouth, MA 02362 Tel: 508-746-1622